D0930813

A Day at the
Beach
Animal Life
on the Shore

Hermit Crabs

by Ellen Lawrence

Consultant:

Professor Steve Hawkins
University of Southampton
Southampton, England

Marine Biological Association
Plymouth, England

BEARPORT
PUBLISHING

New York, New York

Credits

Cover, © Stockforlife/Shutterstock, © Alexander Sviridov/Shutterstock, and © Wil Meinderts/Minden Pictures/FLPA; 2, © Eric Isselee/Shutterstock; 4, © Wil Meinderts/Minden Pictures/FLPA; 5, © Nature Production/Nature Picture Library; 6, © Samuel Kornstein/Shutterstock; 7, © Sue Daly/Nature Picture Library; 8T, © Andrew Burgess/Shutterstock; 8B, © Nicolas Primola/Shutterstock; 9, © Lee Rentz/Alamy; 10T, © imageBROKER/Alamy; 10B, © chl23/Shutterstock; 11, © Nature Photographers Ltd/Alamy; 12, © Ekkapan Poddamrong/Shutterstock; 13, © Iammotos/Shutterstock; 13BL, © Biosphoto/Alamy; 14, © A & J Visage/Alamy; 15, © Michael Mantke/Shutterstock; 16, © D P Wilson/FLPA; 17, © Solvin Zankl/Nature Picture Library; 18, © Nadya Chetah/Shutterstock; 19, © Jane Burton/Nature Picture Library; 20, © Georgette Douwa/Nature Picture Library; 21, © Flonline/FLPA; 22L, © Picturist90/Shutterstock; 22R, © media point inc/Shutterstock; 23TL, © Arnstein Ronning; 23TC, © antos777/Shutterstock; 23TR, © Sue Daly/Nature Picture Library; 23BL, © Sakkarin Kamutsri/Shutterstock; 23BC, © Napat/Shutterstock; 23BR, © Dirk M. de Boer/Shutterstock.

Publisher: Kenn Goin
Senior Editor: Joyce Tavolacci
Creative Director: Spencer Brinker
Photo Researcher: Ruth Owen Books

Library of Congress Cataloging-in-Publication Data

Names: Lawrence, Ellen, 1967– , author.
Title: Hermit crabs / by Ellen Lawrence.
Description: New York, New York : Bearport Publishing, 2018. | Series: A day at the beach : animal life on the shore | Includes bibliographical references and index. | Audience: Ages 5 to 8.
Identifiers: LCCN 2017048991 (print) | LCCN 2017052124 (ebook) | ISBN 9781684025039 (Ebook) | ISBN 9781684024452 (library)
Subjects: LCSH: Hermit crabs—Juvenile literature.
Classification: LCC QL444.M33 (ebook) | LCC QL444.M33 L394 2018 (print) | DDC 595.3/87—dc23
LC record available at *https://lccn.loc.gov/2017048991*

Copyright © 2018 Bearport Publishing Company, Inc. All rights reserved. No part of this publication may be reproduced in whole or in part, stored in any retrieval system, or transmitted in any form or by any means, electronic, mechanical, photocopying, recording, or otherwise, without written permission from the publisher.

For more information, write to Bearport Publishing Company, Inc., 45 West 21st Street, Suite 3B, New York, New York 10010. Printed in the United States of America.

10 9 8 7 6 5 4 3 2 1

Contents

A Big Fight!

Whack! Smack! Thump!

On a rocky shore, two hermit crabs are wrestling.

The crabs are fighting over a large, empty snail shell.

First one crab grabs the shell, then the other pulls it away.

What's so special about the shell?

hermit crab

Hermit crabs belong to a group of animals called crustaceans. Most crustaceans live in water and have an **exoskeleton**. Crabs, lobsters, and shrimp are all crustaceans.

4

These hermit crabs are fighting over a shell.

Borrowed Shell

Unlike most crabs, a hermit crab's body is not completely covered by a hard exoskeleton.

The back half of its body, or **abdomen**, is soft.

To protect it, a hermit crab uses a shell from another sea animal, such as a whelk.

As the crab grows, it swaps its shell for a larger one.

Sometimes, two hermit crabs fight over the same shell!

whelk shell

crab's exoskeleton

How do you think a hermit crab keeps its shell attached to its body?

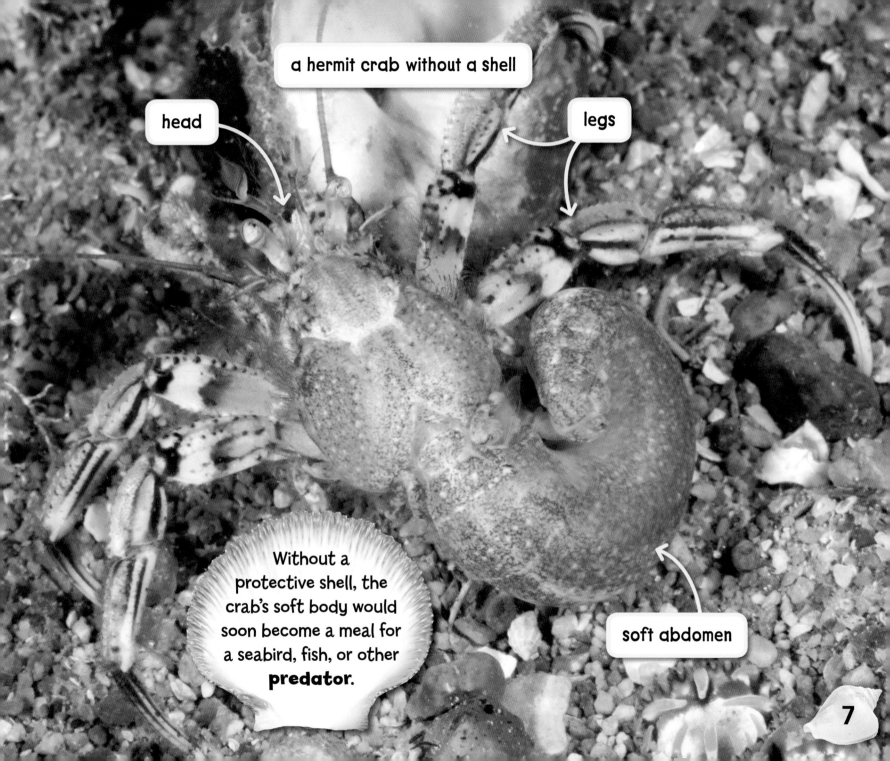

a hermit crab without a shell

head

legs

Without a protective shell, the crab's soft body would soon become a meal for a seabird, fish, or other **predator**.

soft abdomen

7

Legs and More Legs

A hermit crab has five pairs of legs!

Its two large front legs have claws, which are used for fighting and gathering food.

It has two additional pairs of legs that are used for walking.

Its fourth and fifth pairs of legs are tiny.

They hold the crab's body inside its shell.

claws

abdomen

This diagram shows the crab's abdomen curled up inside the shell.

If a predator comes near, a hermit crab quickly tucks itself inside its shell. It blocks the shell's opening with its claws.

a crab tucked safely inside its shell

claws

A Hermit Crab's World

There are more than 1,000 different types of hermit crabs.

Some are smaller than a pea, while others are the size of a coconut.

There are hermit crabs that spend their whole lives in the ocean.

Others make their homes on beaches and in tidal pools.

Still other hermit crabs live on land in tropical places.

Ecuadorian hermit crab

An Ecuadorian hermit crab is smaller than a dime.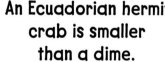

tentacles

sea anemone

Sometimes, a sea anemone will make its home on the shell of an ocean hermit crab. The anemone's stinging tentacles help keep predators away. In return for this protection, the anemone shares the crab's food.

hermit crab

Breathing

All hermit crabs have body parts called gills, which they use to breathe.

Hermit crabs that live in the ocean use their gills to get **oxygen** from the water.

Hermit crabs that live on land also need water to breathe.

These crabs keep their gills moist in order to take in oxygen.

a hermit crab underwater

What kinds of food do you think a hermit crab eats?

Land hermit crabs splash water on their gills to keep them moist. Sometimes, they carry around a supply of water in their shells.

a hermit crab wetting its gills in a tidal pool

gills

13

Hungry Hermits

Some ocean hermit crabs feed on tiny sea animals and plants called **plankton**.

Others graze on seaweed.

Land hermit crabs will eat almost anything!

They chomp on leaves and fruit from seashore trees.

They also eat dead fish, rotting seaweed, and even poop!

a hermit crab eating a turtle egg

A hermit crab has two pairs of antennae, or feelers. The long antennae are used for touching and feeling. The short pair are used for smelling and tasting.

long antenna

short antenna

two pairs of arm-like mouthparts used for holding and tearing food

Baby Crabs

When it's time to **mate**, male and female hermit crabs meet up in the sea.

After mating, the female crab lays thousands of eggs in the water.

Tiny crabs called zoeas (ZOH-ee-uhz) hatch from the eggs.

The zoeas swim in the ocean and feed on plankton.

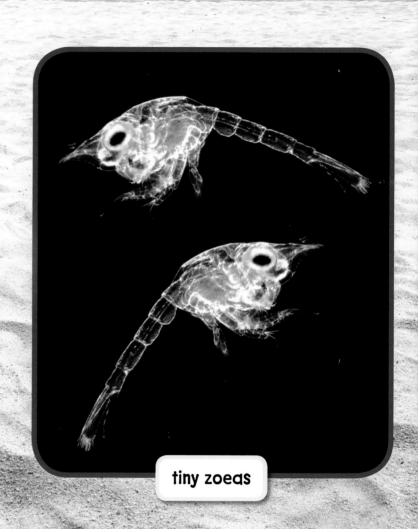

tiny zoeas

As it grows, a baby crab's body also changes shape. It regularly sheds its old exoskeleton, which is replaced by a new, bigger one. Eventually, the crab looks just like a miniature version of its parents.

a young hermit crab without a shell

What do you think a baby hermit crab must do as it gets bigger?

First Shell

Even a baby hermit crab needs a shell—or it could soon become a predator's dinner!

The little crab chooses a small shell to be its first home.

However, as its body grows, the shell gets too tight.

Then the little crab must find a new, bigger shell.

baby hermit crab

Once a crab finds a new shell, it pulls its abdomen from the old one. Then, holding onto the new shell with its front legs, it slides inside.

new, larger shell

hermit crab

old shell

How do you think hermit crabs find and choose their new homes?

19

Time to Swap!

Sometimes, a crab tries out a new shell and discovers it's too big.

Then other hermit crabs that need new shells gather around.

They form a line—from biggest to smallest.

The crab at the head of the line takes the big, empty shell.

Then all the other crabs swap shells down the line—new homes for everyone!

hermit crabs gathering to change shells

On some beaches, there are not enough shells for all the hermit crabs. That's when the crabs get creative! A hermit crab might use a nutshell or a plastic cup to be its home.

red plastic cup

21

Science Lab

Be a Hermit Crab Scientist!

Scientists have studied hermit crabs for many years. Now it's your turn to investigate! Read the following questions and write your answers in a notebook.

I. What do you think the hermit crabs are doing in the picture below?

2. Describe what is happening in these pictures. What do you think the crab is doing and why?

3. Write a paragraph about the life of a hermit crab. Use the words below.

zoea   abdomen   shell

fight   gills   antennae

(The answers are on page 24.)

Science Words

abdomen (AB-duh-muhn) the back part of a crab's body

exoskeleton (eks-oh-SKEL-uh-tuhn) the hard outer covering that protects the bodies of certain animals

mate (MAYT) to come together to produce young

oxygen (OK-suh-juhn) a colorless gas found in air and water that people and animals need to breathe

plankton (PLANGK-tuhn) tiny animals and plants that float in oceans, lakes, and ponds

predator (PRED-uh-tur) an animal that hunts other animals for food

23

Index

Read More

Berne, Emma Carlson. *Crustaceans (My First Animal Kingdom Encyclopedias).* Mankato, MN: Capstone (2017).

Lunis, Natalie. *Crawling Crabs (No Backbone! Marine Invertebrates).* New York: Bearport (2008).

Learn More Online

To learn more about hermit crabs, visit
www.bearportpublishing.com/ADayAtTheBeach

About the Author

Ellen Lawrence lives in the United Kingdom. Her favorite books to write are those about nature and animals. In fact, the first book Ellen bought for herself when she was six years old was the story of a gorilla named Patty Cake that was born in New York's Central Park Zoo.

Answers for page 22

1. The crabs are feeding on a coconut.

2. In the picture on the left, the crab is partly outside its shell. In the picture on the right, the crab has tucked its body inside its shell to stay safe from danger.